The Journey Within

The Journey Within

Dr. Shaifali Gupta

ZORBA BOOKS

ZORBA BOOKS

Publishing Services by Zorba Books, June 2020

Website: www.zorbabooks.com
Email: info@zorbabooks.com
Contact: 0124-4259579/8800509579

Cover design © Sithesh
Copyright © Dr. Shaifali Gupta

Print Book ISBN: 978-93-90011-23-0
Ebook ISBN: 978-93-90011-24-7

The publisher under the guidance and direction of the author has published the contents in this book, and the publisher takes no responsibility for the contents, it's accuracy, completeness, any inconsistencies, or the statements made. The contents of the book do not reflect the opinion of the publisher or the editor. The publisher and editor shall not be liable for any errors, omissions, or the reliability of the contents of the book.

Any perceived slight against any person/s, place or organization is purely unintentional.

Zorba Books Pvt. Ltd. (opc)
Sushant Arcade,
Next to Courtyard Marriot,
Sushant Lok 1, Gurgaon – 122009, India

Acknowledgements

Offered with Love to our Creator, the real author of the book, who I call Sai Baba.

I feel blessed that this book should see the light of the day and would like to express special thanks:

To my husband Dr. Amit Gupta and son Ansh Gupta who have taught me valuable lessons and inspired me to pursue my dreams. You mean the world to me.

To my parents in law, Indu and Girdhar Gupta who have been the pillars of my life; Dr. Sumit Gupta for your encouragement.

To my amazingly supportive friends at home and at office who have been there and guided me through my path of life - you may not find your name mentioned here, but the book would not have been possible without you.

To the wonderful Zorba books, Shalini Gupta and her team who transformed my vision of this book into reality.

And most of all, to my wonderful parents Ashok and Manju Singhal who have taught me the first lessons of life and made me the person I am today; to my loyal brother Harshit Singhal and his wife Prerna for your energy, enthusiasm and faith in the book.

Thank you all for being there and being so motivating!

Contents

1. The Mysterious Stranger

"And how did this happen? By oversight??", Isha was shouting at a colleague in her office. She felt terrible after this. She came back home early today as she experienced an unusual weakness since afternoon. She had called her husband Jai too, who drove her to emergency care at the hospital, frantically suspecting the worst. A thorough check up revealed uncontrolled diabetes bordering on diabetic coma.

She saw Jai sitting on the sofa near the bed in front of her. Lying on the hospital bed, she remembered the day she had met him for the first time, twelve years ago.

Isha was in her first year of college. She had bunked the Organic Chemistry class to go to the college fest at her friend Rashmi's college. She had worn a red silk gown. She had reached the venue about half an hour ago, but could not locate Rashmi. The evening music function was about to begin. Suddenly, she spotted Rashmi with a senior, Jai, who had just won the JAM competition. Although the two of them were talking, Isha noticed that Jai was glancing at Isha every now and then. She walked up to them and introduced herself.

The moment Jai's eyes met Isha's, she felt a strange sort of connection with him. It was as if they had known each other for a long time and the sensation was electrifying.

Within a few minutes into the conversation, Jai was talking about his new job offer at Ernst and Young and how excited he was that the first step of his career was so promising. She was happy for him and shared her dream of biking across North America and of being a social activist to help people.

Isha had gotten busy with her exams immediately after that and then heard that Jai had moved to New York for his internship. Jai later shared that he had found her extremely grounded, settled and chilled out.

Jerking herself off from her dreamy recollections, *Isha wondered what had led her here?*

A mother of two. A software professional working in a corporate. Staying in Mumbai. Workplace not close to home. Isha, at thirty-five, had her hands full.

She was always running, hurrying to reach, to complete, to conform to all the expectations everyone had of her. Expectations at work, from her boss, her colleagues, her kids, her husband, herself, her in-laws and her parents. She was always fulfilling everybody's expectations. She lived by the rules and pushed herself to reach the finish line for the unending tasks everyday. What did she really accomplish in the entire day, she wondered, just pushing herself to complete one task after another.

Although she rarely had a quiet moment, whenever she sat down with herself, she felt the need to stop and analyze where she was going. She wanted to shed off the load she seemed to be carrying—the baggage of memories, desires, regrets, fears, and insecurities. She did not realise that accepting premises of others and adopting belief systems of all around her without analysis had made her thoughts an undecipherable jargon to comprehend.

In a particularly reflective moment she realized she had become extremely defensive.

She had no time to appreciate what was around her or within her. She had been happy and secure earlier. She wondered when she had trapped herself in a bubble of insecurity and walled herself inside. She had erected big defences around herself. If anyone criticized her, it would consume her entire mental space. The thoughts left no space for any sort of contemplation and self-reflection. She had started ignoring herself.

Isha remembered her childhood. She was born in Pune, a mid-sized town, a three-hour drive from Mumbai. Her mother had been one of the kindest people she had ever met. Her father was a perfectionist. They had been simple people. Both of them had done their best. The best they could. The best they knew. They loved her and thought she was perfect. Today, she realized that there was so much of them in her. Growing up, she was such a nice kid, so complete within herself. She had been good at studies and had no sense of competition. She had never hurt anyone and was a very considerate person. As a youngster, she had always been ready to offer help to any person who needed it, everyone's favourite confidant. She had loved singing and always had a song on her lips and a smile on the face.

After finishing her graduation in computer science, she had come to Mumbai for a job. She realised that this city had a life, a pace of its own and one had to be on the run to keep pace with it. She had time and energy on her side and loved the fast pace of the city. This is where she had met Jai again. They worked in the same office. She liked his style of leadership, his honesty, and his sense of humor. They seemed to connect at many levels and there was so much they had to share with each other. Visits, phone calls, emails, and text messages started passing back and forth more frequently.

He had not just brought fun to her life but also love, romance, passion and a deep sense of fulfillment. Jai had an amazing sense of humour. They laughed easily together and the dates were always a lot of fun. Love unfolded naturally out of this beautiful friendship. She had always known that they would be perfect for each other. So, when Jai and her parents suggested that they get married, she was happy to take the dive. Jai was incredibly romantic and the initial years of marriage were a dream. New work, its challenges, the fun time exploring restaurants and theatres, trying out new recipes, being pampered by in-laws and parents, life had passed by in a happy rush.

Soon after they got married, they had Ria. She was a bundle of joy to have around. Isha had to return to work just 6 weeks after Ria's birth, and Jai had been there to help her babysit and shuttle Ria around and even bottle feed her while Isha would be busy replying to emails or answering work phone calls. Her office was at the other end of Mumbai which required her to travel an hour and a half to reach the workplace. The initial years passed by prancing around her. Isha was occasionally overwhelmed by expectations from home and work. But Jai had been there during the challenging and confusing time of new motherhood, giving a helping hand and being there for her and doing the odd jobs too. Before she knew it, it was time for Ria to start playschool. It was around this time that Isha went through one of the most traumatic events of her life.

In a quirk of fate, Isha had lost her younger sister. Although they were two years apart, Sia had always been her best friend. They had been so close that everyone teased them about being Siamese twins. Their parents used to joke that the two of them were stuck together. But as they had grown older, they had chosen separate paths, and had different destinies. Sia had been like a second inner voice to her. After Sia's death, she felt as if she was always on autopilot. She had no friends and zero social life. At some point, she had stopped speaking to herself too. She struggled with making friends. It was as if she was just drifting through life and did not really care for anything.

She was juggling all her responsibilities and trying to perform all her roles to the utmost perfection. She had gotten used to pushing herself to get the immediate task done. Her job was a place to spend the hours of the day rather than a place to express her best. Occasionally though, at some level, she was questioning and trying to make sense of the beliefs, perceptions and the philosophies that she was overfilled with.

"When have I truly appreciated myself for who I am?" she thought, suddenly irritated with herself. Settling down in the chair after the morning rush, she found herself in a pensive mood. Her sugar levels would shoot up often and she suffered from chronic backache that would often make it difficult for her to complete daily chores. Although, she still attended to the household chores as best as she could, it meant ignoring her body's call to care for herself.

What were the things that had changed within her since her childhood days? She couldn't understand how it could all be different.

A sound from outside her cubicle jerked her attention back to the computer screen. Her inbox was overflowing with mails. She double clicked the refresh button on the computer screen and saw numerous red lettered unread mails roll out on the screen.

Suddenly, after all the years, she felt the need to understand the premise that defined her existence. What had she started out to do in her life? Why was she here? She was overwhelmed by the feeling that this couldn't be all. Life could not be so meaningless, there must be a bigger purpose to existence.

She was searching for answers. She wanted somebody to guide her, to help her get started on this journey to the unknown. Somehow, she felt that this need had to be addressed within herself. Something told her that the answers to her search lay within her.

That night she lay on her bed thinking. She wondered, "Where do I look for answers?" Jai and the kids had gone to sleep.

She was unusually restless and sleep seemed a far way off. She got up, walked into the adjacent room, and sat down with her diary. It was difficult to focus on her thoughts, so she got up again and made herself a cup of tea. She returned to the living room, picked up her diary and went out into the balcony. It was a quiet night, although a bit chilly. She plopped herself down into the chair and glanced up at the starlit sky. It was a clear night and she could spot all the different constellations.

Her mind was looking around for answers. Lost in her thoughts, she suddenly felt as if she was not the only one present in the balcony. She stared intently at the figure materializing in front of her. She did not feel any fear at the sudden intrusion, instead she found herself curious about this mysterious presence. Luxuriant curls framed his handsome face. His dark eyes were deep and had a child's transparency. She was astonished to see this radiant person, with eyes sparkling with love and the hint of a gentle smile on his lips, standing in front of her.

He had not been there moments ago. Where had he come from? She wondered, "Am I imagining things now?" It was night time but she had never experienced something like this earlier. Her scientific mind was in no mood to give in to supernatural theories. She was about to scream for help but something stopped her. She wanted to stay there and ask him about his identity. There was a strange serenity on his face. He seemed to be all flesh but there was radiance around him.

He was casually dressed in a grey t-shirt and jeans. She noticed that the t-shirt had a small patch torn off on the right sleeve. His face was serene with an almost palpable glow around him. His eyes were deep and loving, simple and approachable. They twinkled with clarity and seemed to radiate more light than the stars at which she had been staring. His face did have some wrinkles but glowed with a tranquil beauty she had never seen before. There was something regal about his presence. She felt hypnotised by what appeared before her and developed an instant liking for him. An indescribable peace permeated through her as she glanced at him.

"Who are you?" she gasped. He smiled in reply. His silence intrigued Isha. She did not know how to interpret it, much like a young child watching the magician.

"Do you have a name? How do I address you?" she asked again, surprised by her own question.

"Don't have one. You can call me Cookie. Does that work for you?"

"That sounds too weird. Can you choose something more normal …some name I could relate to. Who are you?" she repeated her question.

It was as if she could not proceed without knowing the person's identity. "I'll call you Sai", she said. The words escaped her even before she knew what they meant. She thought he nodded as if in confirmation. In a moment of illumination, she realized that she was encountering her Self, her guide within.

"How did you come here?" she asked, bewildered.

"Space and time are just a playground. I have always been here," the stranger replied.

"Interesting," she thought. Her mind was flooded with questions. As she was articulating her next question, she realised that he had disappeared again. Was this a joke?

"When the student is ready, the teacher appears," Sai whispered.

"Where are you now?" she had almost let out a scream.

"Sitting inside you," she heard him from somewhere within her.

"What is going on? She could feel a change within her body even before she completed the question. She felt her gut twist within. Her heart skipped a beat as if it needed to make space for him.

She closed her eyes to assimilate the experience. She straightened her face, shoulders and her spine as if she needed to extend herself to give him space. Somehow, she was happy he had come. She knew she had a lot of questions for him. There was a long distance to go till she found her long forgotten path.

She intended to ask the Master all the questions that had weighed on her all these years. She was looking forward to the new task at hand.

2. Discovering the Thought Machine

'Your mind is an instrument, a tool. It is there to be used for a specific task, and when the task is completed, you lay it down.'

– Eckhart Tolle

As she settled back into her bed, she heard an affectionate voice.

"Hey Isha, I am inside your mind and watching the thoughts connect and form linkages. This mind, or the 'thought machine' of yours is overworked and unregulated. I could help you clean it up."

"Do you mean this can actually be cleaned up?"

Isha was astonished by the suggestion. "Sai," she pleaded, concealing her uncertainty, "could you take over the machine for a day and just clean it up and service it?"

"No, Isha. I want you to step back with me and see yourself for some time."

"Sit and stare at yourself," Sai said, "without a mirror."

I could be standing and working too, Isha thought. It did not come easily initially. But as she got the hang of it, she started to enjoy the experience. She decided to watch herself that day. Life is so dynamic and beautiful and fun. Stepping back to look at herself seemed to be a lot of fun. It was initially peaceful. She realized she could work more with less going on within her. But soon she observed herself reacting to a situation. She watched herself through the entire episode. Was it required? She had no answers yet. She noticed that she was easily irritated and this prompted her to react negatively. If she could stop herself at that moment and talk to her heart, fill it with love and then act, things would be completely different.

Yesterday, she had been talking to her friend at the office about looking good physically. Her friend had been arguing that looking good physically makes us feel good about ourselves.

True. But how many of us care to look at our inner selves every day? Is that not as important? Would it not also make us feel good about ourselves?

That night, Isha felt as she was being guided closer to nature. She was on the terrace. It was a full moon night. The moonlight was brilliant in its radiance. She was prompted to spend the entire night on the terrace.

Life suddenly felt different with Sai inside her. There was a new serenity around her. While she was reflecting on these sudden and new changes inside her, someone rushed to her and gave her a hug. She looked down at her daughter and smiled. Jai, her husband, had finished a telephonic conversation and joined them. He put on some music while the children started playing on the terrace. She felt as if the whole universe was an elegantly orchestrated symphony.

Isha 's thoughts wandered back to just a few weeks ago. She realized it had been a long time since they had enjoyed a moonlit night together. Generally, they would just sit in front of the television with their dinner.

"Wow! Wow! Wow! Sai, this is so simple," Isha exclaimed.

"Where are you? What is so simple?" Jai queried, almost in a whisper.

Sensing that she needed to share further so that Jai was on the same page as her, she opened her heart and shared her recent experiences with him. Though she felt liberated from the stress that personified her previous life, she wondered whether she could spend the rest of her life at home and at workplace with the new found equanimity. She also wondered if the new found equanimity would decrease her enthusiasm towards work at her office and home. She reminisced of her interest in writing and how she had abandoned it when the study load and the distractions at college had taken most of her time.

As they ventured deeper into the night with melodious music and rejuvenating moonlight around, her reflections of the past were interrupted by the beauty of the present moment. They heard some melodious songs and enjoyed the pleasant breeze, clicked selfies with the moon, laughed and sang some of their favourite songs.

After she had put the kids to sleep, Isha spent time looking within. She knew there was a lot of cleaning up to do. Over the years, she had adopted many thoughts and belief systems from her social environment. These had been embedded inside her so deeply that it would take a lot of work before she was able to entirely rid herself of this social conditioning.

The sources of inputs of her thoughts were unregulated. The thought chains were being formed quickly and at random. Sai elaborated, "These thought chains define your actions, personality, and character. They affect your sense of peace and joy in life. Why do you let this process of thought linkage and connections be unsupervised?"

The chains were old and rusty. They were deeply ingrained in her physical self. Sai's mere presence in her inner space seemed to make these thoughts less rusty and more aligned.

Isha fell asleep lost in her thoughts.

❁ ❁ ❁

3. Oiling Life with Love

"Life is love and love is life."

> – *Nisargadatta Maharaj,*
> *an Indian sage.*

"A lot of oiling is required," she heard Sai saying as she woke up, "Do you mean the oil of unconditional love and non-judgement," Isha enquired still sleepy.

"Yes," she heard the voice within her whisper to her soothingly, "Love is the oil that lubricates your thought machine. You have to oil your parts regularly. Stay open to new experiences in each moment. Your thought machine is so overworked that it has no time to revel in the joys manifesting around you all the time. Drown yourself in the fountain of love within you."

"All the negativity would melt in the brilliant light of love. Love is the eternal never-ending gift to ourselves and others," Isha was now beginning to understand.

Whenever we have a negative thought, we drain ourselves of energy. These thoughts are so powerful. Each thought has repercussions. Happy and loving thoughts result in happy and fulfilling people and circumstances. A thought which is disconnected from love is a wasted thought. Our thoughts create our circumstances, our present and future.

"Good morning Jai," Isha greeted her husband enthusiastically. Adorning his tall frame was a deep blue robe with a red T-shirt and shorts within. He was standing beside her with twinkling eyes. Isha offered him warm water with lemon and honey and smiled at his inquisitiveness. Turning to him, she said softly, "I am beginning to realise how precious our thoughts and our thought machine is. The thought machine i.e. our mind is the means by which we can manifest our dreams. We can manifest whatever we desire. For this to happen, they need to be coherent and continuous so that the universe is able to decipher them. Thoughts interspersed with negativity, doubt, worry, mistrust nullify the strength of the positive thoughts, our dreams." Isha paused as if surprised at her own discovery.

Physical vitality and energy followed the changes in Isha's attitude. The sickly pallor with dark circles that characterised her face was replaced by glowing skin and shimmering health. She was starting to cherish life and was learning to see each incident as a divine personalised lesson to learn something from.

The magic of the inner journey had started to work its miracles on her.

Jai and Isha relaxed in their slightly cluttered study room. They were staring at the fun family picture on the wall and both started to laugh at the memory of the prank they had played while on their holiday to Bali. Giggling, Isha realised that Jai had not lost the innate ability to know how to make her laugh.

Their work took a lot of their time away from each other. Lately, Isha found herself wanting to spend more time with him. It was difficult to find time for each other because of their high-pressure jobs and the countless household chores that never seemed to end. Perhaps, she could try and make up by texting and calling him more often.

Feeling relaxed lately, they had consciously started to open up and share their thoughts with each other. They had promised each other that they would hear each other out patiently. They learnt together that love was a verb, and they had come to learn the meaning of 'unconditional' through an interesting journey together. 'Unconditional' meant loving the other just as they were, instead of insisting on forcing their expectations on each other. They had learnt to give each other space to grow but had also learnt to accept each other without trying to change anything in each other. This had made it possible for them to begin on their journey to love each other unconditionally. Despite their busy schedules, they had recently started spending more time with each other and she was happy that they were on this journey together.

Discussing her thoughts with Jai, she shared, "The motive behind every single action for all of us was love."

He continued animatedly," The love of myself and my relationships, possessions and so on."

"Yes," Isha thought loudly, "This 'me' may be small or may embrace the whole universe. Love can heal and inspire and bring us closer to our higher Universal Self."

"And we need to treat ourselves with lots of love. All the hurtful thoughts stored within us need to be released with love and forgiveness."

Our thoughts, she was now learning, settled in the body and manifested themselves physically. All the thought loops were interconnected and replicated at a very fast rate.

She understood that the responsibility of the input and output of the thought-mind-body machine was hers. As Sai helped her remove the older, deeper thought chains of social conditioning within her, the newer thought chains of judgemental thoughts started breaking apart. Unable to find the loops with which to connect, the newly appearing judgemental thoughts floated off no longer settling within Isha.

They sat outside in the balcony together, with their steaming cups of tea and smiled at each other. Isha was glad that he understood her.

❀ ❀ ❀

4. Mind as a Mastermind

"To the mind that is still, the whole universe surrenders"

– Lao Tzu

She realised that we were so obsessed with our thoughts and problems. Lately, she concluded it had little to do with external circumstances. It was the basic nature of the mind to be preoccupied with some thought. She recollected an incident in the *Mahabharata*. Arjun, Krishna's brother-in-law, was one of his closest friends. If Krishna had wanted, he could have transformed Arjun's wayward mind to an illumined mind so that Arjun could act resolutely in a moment of crisis. However, he only guided Arjun. Krishna had advised Arjun that he could only rid himself from his ignorance through his own efforts.

It is only possible to reach Truth through an internal struggle with untruth. Truth, thus achieved, will be a lasting treasure, Isha thought.

This morning too, Isha found herself awake at 5 o'clock. She promised to accept all people and

"

circumstances in her life today exactly as they were. It was as if the undesirable habit of procrastination had been cauterized. She felt a surge of enthusiasm inside her and was learning to see life as a magical adventure. It was as if the grooves in her brain had filled themselves with love towards herself and the world around her. She smiled softly. The noise had slowly started to fade away. The cloud of thoughts that followed her generally seemed to have thinned out today.

Our mind is so loaded with subconscious thoughts. These thoughts are often random, repetitive, and irrelevant to the many situations in which we find ourselves. Repetition strengthens them so much that they distort the true scenario. We are constantly on this roller coaster thought ride because we identify ourselves only with our thoughts. We have to learn that we were the masters of this roller coaster called mind. We need to assume responsibility and then we can choose whether to move it or keep it stationary.

She recollected a story about Buddha that she had heard years ago. Once, Buddha had been walking with his friend. This was before he gained enlightenment. A fly sat on his shoulder. Unthinkingly, he swatted it away with his hand. He stopped and repeated the same action. His friend asked him why he had done that. He had explained that the first time he had not realized what he had done. The first time, the action had been done subconsciously without conscious awareness, just as we let thoughts come into us without our knowledge and let them become a part of us our belief systems. Consequently, they become a part of our personality. We act without thinking about our actions. Buddha was constantly watching his thoughts and actions and wanted to be completely aware and thus, responsible for himself.

It's foolish to let ideas and concepts picked up from external sources, either from belief systems, social attitudes or preconceived insecurities, inform and control our life. The only way to rise above our thoughts is to recognise the thought machine as a tool. The next step is to see ourselves as a master of this machine and command it to churn thoughts of love and oneness always, and to reprimand it when it slips from its duty. How can we let it control us instead of us controlling it? It is like a demon on the run when we let our mind define and run our lives without giving it the monistic perspective.

"You must have heard the story of the giant who needed his owner to assign him some work at all times otherwise he would end up eating the owner. The owner having exhausted with all the tasks, scared for his life, ran to the Master for help. The Master advised him to set the giant the task of counting the sand particles on the shore. Our mind is that powerhouse. It is the giant without a task. We need to give it some worthwhile work to do," Sai said, "become a Master-mind."

She understood the words she had come across earlier with greater clarity. Isha realised that the Master's advice was correct. She was always judging herself and the world around her, judging to verify if the world conformed to her standards. If only she could let go of this need to define herself and the world around her.

We are all part of the same consciousness and we could share so much joy if we could only let go of the need to judge or conform. We are Consciousness beyond thought, and whenever we connect with it the joy is complete. No thoughts are worthy of the joy of the thoughtless state when you connect within.

Sai continued, "One has to recognise the fundamental Truth-the principle of Universal Consciousness. It is within you, a part of the whole. It is possible to know this only through the intellect, by using the thought machine, because it alone has the capacity to discriminate. The intellect should help us in discernment, ensuring that we are able to recognise whether our choices are right or wrong.

Excited by her newfound knowledge, she said, "Sai, I did not realize that I can guide my thoughts and choose my perspective. I did not know that thoughts are a means to an end. I can choose to feel stressed or relaxed. I am beginning to realise what is inside me can be independent of my external circumstances. I can actually direct the external circumstances by choosing to be in control of the thought machine."

The thoughts that she had were her decisions and responsibility. She could not imagine that she had chosen such confused and negative thoughts to make her life.

Before starting on this journey of self-realization, Isha used to find concentrating on her breath even for a moment such a Herculean task. Random thoughts would bombard her for attention. Lately, though, she was able to observe them as they passed through her mind, while concentrating on her breath. She felt the pleasant air touching her nostrils. Her facial muscles relaxed. She was now breathing deeply and felt a faint smile on her lips. The sun was up in the sky and everything was bright and clear in the balcony. Tranquillity descended over her.

As the thoughts loosen their hold on the mind, there are gaps in the dense cloud of incessant thinking. These gaps are the times when we experience our Self; our expanse, beauty, truth. As we learn to concentrate on the Self, we stop responding to the attention seekers in us—thoughts, emotions, external situations. We feel liberated. We revel in this experience as the frequency of these experiences increases. This helps us recognize the mind and its activity. There is an immediate relaxation in our lives. Soon, the frequency of these gaps and the duration of these gaps increases. Our emotional drama, the negativity with which we surround ourselves and others, decreases. Life is suddenly relatively smoother and more effortless than before. Whenever the mind finds an opportunity, it comes back with a vengeance wanting attention and the energy for the time it lost out.

I guess, now I am more equipped to handle it, Isha thought.

It was a Sunday. This peace that she was experiencing was so complete she wanted to do nothing that would disturb it. There was still the cooking to be done. Isha went into the kitchen. She cooked some sprouts and sprinkled some freshly chopped vegetables for lunch and got herself a refreshing strawberry shake from the refrigerator.

She walked to the bed where her daughter, Ria, was drawing on a paper by herself. Her twinkling eyes danced with energy and joy at almost everything she did. Everyone in the room wanted to talk to her whenever she was around. She was always learning new things. Although she was very talkative, Ria was also a devoted listener. She would never feel hurt if she was told something she did not like. Everything was for the moment. She would immediately shift to something equally fun and interesting. She could make a doll out of a stick and it was amazing to see how many games she could create from just about anything.

Ria taught her so many lessons every day. Ria had an empty mind but she was ever busy and learning and growing each moment. Isha knew that she had her greatest teacher in her children. Ria had taught her that there was no carryover baggage from this moment to the next. Each moment had its own beauty, honesty, freshness and happiness. There was only love which we could tap into and absorb.

Isha no longer had to remind herself of Sai's presence within or search or wait for him. She would see him each time she closed her eyes and her words would echo within her whenever she was contemplating something.

"Each interaction with a person should be a fresh interaction. Greet the soul when you see a person. See each individual without his mental constructions," Sai shared, as Isha stared at Ria subconsciously learning the new lessons.

Isha realized she needed a quiet mind. She needed to be mindful of her thoughts and not allow stray thoughts to take root.

Sai told her, "Only the seeds of divine bliss should find space in your mind. A well-concentrated mind can see the nature of things much more deeply. You need to strengthen your mind machine for it to work for you. Small practices each day will make it strong."

She decided to do mental housekeeping every morning. This would allow her to align her perspective on a regular basis. Just as we need to clean up, reorganize our room, or our workstation, we need to reorganize our thoughts on a daily basis. Isha understood that random thoughts, which may have entered into the mind, needed to be attended to, sorted and settled.

As you start understanding the thought machine, you realize that it slips so fast. Whenever you are not looking, it slips off to do its own dance on you. It makes your life into a puppet-show. It was a continuous responsibility and the easiest way to tame it was to surrender it to God completely. Physically, it meant connecting inside with a name and form. It meant always being aware of His presence within yourself and within others around you.

As she closed her eyes, Isha saw an eagle perched on top of a building. Sai was sitting on the eagle and asked her to sit on it as well. As soon as she sat on the eagle, it started to fly slowly. It couldn't fly very high because of their combined weight, so they circled in the sky not very far off the ground.

Being aware of her breath was so serene. It was intoxicating. She experienced the cool fresh air of joy entering her to meet Sai within and accumulated negativity moving out with each breath.

She also realized that whenever she was angry or upset, her breathing would become shallow. All it took to calm herself down was concentrating on her breath, in order to bring it back to the normal rhythm.

Focusing on our breath gives us the chance to control our mind and access the universal energy, she thought.

"Love is the fundamental principle of life. Fill your lives with love. Live in Love," Sai remarked with angelic tenderness.

But this love had to be unconditional. She remembered Dhristrashtra, Duryodhana's father and the king of Indraprastha. His attachment to Duryodhana had blinded him. This conditional love had been the cause of all the sorrow in his life and for those around him. Had he been aligned to the Universal intelligence and reprimanded Duryodhana, the great battle of Kurukshetra would not have happened. If our actions were governed with love and had pure motive, there would be no battles in our lives either. Isha smiled at her enlightened thought.

Sai continued, "When you love, let love be your complete entity. Being love means getting rid of all your baggage. Feel the love for the creator within and without you. Know that love is the energy on which this universe is based. Love crosses all boundaries of time and space. It truly knows no boundaries. Feel this love within you and you speak to the creator for this is the language of the creator."

❀ ❀ ❀

5. Isha's Journey to Mindfulness

Isha dreamt Sai sitting within her and as she tried to reach him from the outside but the ladder erected blocked her from reaching Sai. Try as she might, she could not enter the inner Sai but she did not give up. She realized the ladder that she had seen was the ladder of unending desires.

Waking up, Isha thought about how much her life had changed in the last few months. She realized that she had never really enjoyed the moment. She was perennially elsewhere, trapped in her thoughts. Whenever she was with Ria, even though Ria wanted to share everything with her, she was unable to fully enjoy Ria's presence. "Mummy, are you listening to me?" her daughter would demand. "Of course, I am," Isha would reply, while stealing a glance in the mirror. "Mumma, look here," Ria would insist. Isha was with her and not with her completely.

In the office, she was always more comfortable if she had things to do than just talk to the person in front of her. Even though she was present, her attention would always be divided. She knew that her attention span had decreased since her school days. She could not have cleared her exams with this concentration span. Her thought world was filled with thoughts and expectations of what happened and what should have happened. She was always thinking about the past and future but never about the present. It was as if she had promised herself never to stay in the present.

How could I ever have felt happy? She wondered now thinking about her old self.

We need to put down our thought baggage, of the past, of the future, to be able to relate to the present, she thought.

"Our presence is required in the present," she chuckled to herself.

She started relating more with people around her. She also remembered Sai often.

We need to love ourselves first-mentally, physically, emotionally. We need to treat ourselves with sensitivity and remember that everything was a part of the same energy. It is so important to connect to the Love within, and immerse ourselves in that Love.

In life, we are always rushing around trying to fulfil expectations. We're so busy doing this that we deprive ourselves of the love and energy we need the most, in order to connect deeply with ourselves. If you have given enough love and been open in the present moment, there can never be anxiety about the future.

Whenever we are immersed in this feeling of love, we are in a position to bank on the Divine Energy.

In just a few days after Sai took over the control of the thought machine, she felt transformed. A life-long burden seemed to be lifting from her.

Sai was enjoying being inside Isha. He had always been there, but now Isha had willingly transferred all her burden.

Liberation from stressful life does not require any outer renunciations. What is needed is inner renunciation of your ties, desires, and attachments.

She had begun to feel guided since Sai had entered her mind space.

"But wasn't He within each one of us all the time?" Isha wanted to ask everyone she met now.

He wasn't there to fulfil our whims or fancies. He was there to share the view, the higher perspective.

Isha had recently ventured out of her cocoon and confided her journey in Ami, her colleague at the office. Being in her company made her feel joyous, exhilarated and carefree. She was surprised to discover that amazing friends were there around us, whenever we opened our hearts to them.

"We were often so full of ourselves," she shared with Ami at the office during lunch hour.

"Self-forgetfulness is so necessary." Ami added.

"But we were so full of our problems, our miseries that we had no time to look beyond the tiny worlds we have locked ourselves into."

"The moment we see beyond our limited selves, or rather looked at our connectedness, our continual need to ask for something disappears and we find ourselves in a constant state of awe towards everything around us. We become thankful for everything around us. The energy, inner connect, if it were to be translated into a feeling, would be a complete immersion in love. This love is all-encompassing. There can be no feeling of insecurity or competitiveness or incompleteness when you breathe in this love."

It is all one and all flows to experience the whole. Nothing on the physical or the mental plane can be locked or stored in one place. The joy of sharing and letting go was uplifting. When you give, surrender completely. Give after connecting within. The love that you share will enfold you and stay with you in times when you need it the most.

The only way any true relationship is possible is when we completely identify with the other person. A real relationship is possible when we connect within and identify that our partner is only an extension of this source. All relationships and people happen in our life because we need to learn from them. Be open and search for clues in the outer world, which push us ahead in the inner journey.

Each moment can be extremely fulfilling if we are open to it without our defences and insecurities. Whenever we interact with another person, we need to greet the soul - the person without mental constructions.

They decided to go for a long trek to the hill on an extended weekend holiday. The fresh mountain air energised their minds and lifted their spirits.

That night at the hotel, Isha was scribbling in her diary,

As I climb the mountains, the scenario changes, the perspective changes, i get a bird's eye view of all that is happening ...

It is difficult to trek, unless you have practiced hard regularly and are seasoned to climb, but the view never fails to astonish. The smaller details disappear and a new vision comes in. The same trees, which were down there, look greener now and are more beautiful. You notice the variety of leaves and the beauty in them. You breathe the air in and breathe the mist out.

You notice the silhouette of trees and the blue sky against it. The birds flying in various patterns. you wonder if there is some hidden message which you are unable to decipher...

The sky seems bluer and clearer than when you saw it from below, you wonder why...

You see the clouds (of your thoughts) below you, you never imagined you could look beyond them when you were down there. Suddenly you realize that they are only a layer and there is a whole new world above it which is greener, more intense and more beautiful. You suddenly notice that you are taking deeper longer breaths than you did earlier. You feel the cold air enter your nostrils and revel in this new sensation that your nostrils feel...

6. Goals and Desires

*"The human mind is a spark of Almighty Consciousness.
Whatever the powerful mind believes very intensely, it
would immediately come to pass."*

– Autobiography of a Yogi

Isha was in the office looking at some excel sheets on the computer. She was still happily reeling under the discovery of the power of the thought machine. She was happy to awaken to the power of her own mind to make magic in her life.

When her friends at Rotary Club had organised a music festival recently, she had volunteered to sing for it and anchor the entire program. She was amazed at the kind of response it got and the thrill she felt in the entire experience. She was now planning to organise a musical parody at the annual function at office too. She was excited about it. Music made her laugh, sing and dance. Programs like these ensured that music was on her mind.

She recalled a job interview she had gone to some years back. After exchanging pleasantries and cordial questions, Isha was asked, "How do you look at the sojourn in this organization?" "I expect myself to learn more each day from all the people I might encounter," she had replied truthfully.

The next question didn't have an easy answer, "What is your aim in life?"

I wish I knew!

"I don't know," she replied, again opening herself completely.

"Well, you should have a goal in your life, right? Otherwise, you will never reach anywhere," the young lady prompted her, "You would just move along curved lines to reach the same place."

"I agree with you," Isha had volunteered. She was surprised that the young lady had surmised something so clearly that had been reflecting in all aspects of her life.

The question had stayed with her even after she left the interview room. She wasn't sure. There had to be a way to know.

It was as if the question had opened Pandora's Box for her.

What was her goal in life? What were desires?
What is the difference between goals and desires?
Which goals were worth pursuing? Which goals or desires, when achieved, would give her satisfaction and fulfilment?

What would help her to deal with the sense of incompleteness that she still felt within her?

The questions came back to her. She wondered if Sai had heard the questions.

In the corporate world, she had seen life's successes being defined by possessions and professional successes evaluated by power over others. Physical acquisitions had been the parameter defined for growth in the world she lived in. She moved around with insecurity, hoarding things, even holding up love which she refused to share.

Isha was again reminded of the strength of the thought machine or the mind. Such a robust thought machine could not be without a purpose. Isha concluded that it obviously had a better use.

"What is its goal?" Isha asked Sai.

She learnt that only gaining inner knowledge was of no use. It had to be put to practice.

"A lump of coal cannot be washed with soap and water or with milk. It has to be burnt in the fire so that it turns to white ash," the benevolent guide shared. "Similarly, only gaining awareness within is not helpful. Only action on the knowledge, working on our flaws continuously and steadily could bring about any change or spiritual wisdom in our lives."

The first step from the outer world to the inner world was the most important one, but once that was taken, it was important to align our actions to the perspective.

Gone was her old cynicism and negativity. She saw she was doing things that she had not done before and felt really motivated and loads of fun.

Recently, Isha had opened herself to newer challenges, personally and professionally, by moving out of the comfort zone. The presence of Sai made it easier. Each day was now filled with more adventure, passion and energy with newer experiences in life.

She was being offered a new project at the office which involved so much of data management and a lot of creative inputs, something she had not worked with earlier but she was excited to be on the new team. Work, at the office, suddenly, was loads of fun now.

She heard Sai's voice when she was discovering new work lessons by herself at the office.

Understanding our source can be our only goal. Let our thoughts be attracted to the Universal Consciousness as iron filings are attracted to the magnet. The Consciousness acts as a magnet to those who surrender to Him. Then, the control of the thought machine doesn't remain such an ardent task. Conscientiously engaged in our work, we should remain immersed in an inward beatitude. During these periods of deeper connection, we find our goals being spoken to us.

These are personal life goals that keep coming back to us even after we brush them away. They give deeper meaning to our lives. Otherwise, we find our lives meaningless as we run around accumulating materialistic things that we do not even need.

Isha had always wanted to write a book. The desire had first manifested in herself when she turned twelve. Her mother had gifted her a diary and said, "In this diary you can write whatever you feel but cannot share with anyone else." Since then, the diary had been her closest companion. She called the diary 'Kitty' as Anne Frank had called her diary. She had started sharing her thoughts with Kitty and realized that the diary had a life of its own. She often found words written which she wanted to hear. Kitty had always guided her, writing 'to' her was hearing her own Self. The process became so beautiful and somewhere along the way, Isha had realized that this was her life's goal, sharing these words. She always knew she would share it, she just didn't know when, and how, she would do so.

Writing was cathartic. It was as if once the words were written down, the lessons could always be revisited. To share was to learn, to remind, to understand. The intent was important and with the right intent, the action was as important and beautiful and fruitful.

A lot of years had passed since she had written in her diary.

"A recurring dream can only be your life's mission," she heard herself speak, "do not push it away. Nurture it, let it grow within you and then consistently work towards it."

Jai was standing close to her. He heard her talking to herself and said, "Yes, irrespective of where and when you start, you are bound to be surprised at the outcome. We are not frustrated when we do not achieve a goal but when we do not have a meaningful goal to achieve."

He couldn't agree more. He had always wanted to be a cricketer and today, he was a state-level cricketer along with being a successful entrepreneur.

He encouraged her, "If we have been given an intention or a dream, we have also been given the time, resources, energy, and skill to fulfil the dream. Pursue your lifetime goal. All these coincidences are your clues. It is as if the universe has come together to make it true."

Isha had known this herself. Whenever she had concentrated on an outer world gift or a position, the journey had been stressful, filled with turbulence. The sense of achievement had disappeared even before she experienced it.

Stand up and walk forward boldly on the path, follow your dreams and your destiny. I will be with you, leading you, guiding you, and bringing you through safely, Sai assured.

But now, she was relaxed and enjoying the journey.

She was using daily opportunities to sparkle, to polish her gifts, to release the chains that she had held so strongly to.

She understood that since she had started listening to Sai, her life was so much fun. She had also observed that her self-esteem had improved, a slight strengthening of will power.

The last time she had spoken to her mother, she had said, "The only thing I want for you is happiness. I hope you are always happy with yourself. I pray for this all the time." She willed happiness each moment. Happiness was a state of mind and had nothing to do with any external circumstances.

How and when had her the mind linked happiness to the external world? Why did the mind not seek conscious approval for the thought linkages? Why did we allow ourselves to be bound to the distorted logic?

The journey of life was meant to be the journey within. But today, it had become an outward journey for most of us. It was the outward goals, prizes, fame and power that mattered. The impact was more important than the real job. The 'likes' and 'fans' were more important than the real message even in the virtual world. Peer acceptance was more important than our own sanity. With the goals lopsided, there was a small chance that the path was right.

She realized that everyone had the same goal—to find happiness, whether those focused on the external or internal world. But the difference lay in how each person defined happiness. Although, power and money made it possible to achieve some things, it had its highs and lows, and these things were transient. The in-between times were interspersed with insecurities and depression.

"When we engage ourselves in activities meaningful to us, we see our frustrations towards life melt away. We can never be wrong if we follow our inner voice. The goal we reach may be different, but it will give us greater happiness and peace. It is important to always remember this," she emphasized, as if to herself, "there are gifts beyond money and fame."

She had discovered that whenever we were in this thought mould, doing our best and following our highest dreams, we inspire others. The happiness and energy that we radiate when we follow our dreams also inspires others, whom we touch in our lives.

Our thoughts define our limits. Reach out to remove them if you don't like them. We limit ourselves, it is only our fears which prevent us from pursuing our dreams.

"Sai, how do I know I am on the right path? Are there any guideposts on this journey to myself?

I cannot always understand whether it is the thought from the thought machine or the inner voice speaking."

"Lord," Isha prayed, "from now on, can you please give me only spiritual gifts—relationships, thoughts, work and returns. Rather, can you give me the absolute power of discrimination?"

What I am asking is absolute control over this thought machine.

7. Universal Synchronicity

"Nothing happens by chance, my friend. No such thing as luck. A meaning behind every little thing, and such a meaning behind this. Part for you, part for me, may not see it all real clear right now, but we will, before long."

– Richard Bach.

When we are connected, we see signs guiding us, unseen forces helping us. The Universal Consciousness communicates through all its manifestations—sharing its awareness and constantly guiding us towards our goals. We see these in the form of sudden flashes, visions, symbols, chance meetings with strangers and subtle changes in our breathing patterns or heart rate. It could be a wisp of wind, a widening of eyes, a slight blink, a relaxed body and sound, a sudden disconnected calm, or even a disconnected thought that you know is not yours. It could be a slip of the tongue, brightening of the scene, a sudden beautiful flower, or a flying bird, Isha thought recalling her experiences.

Sai prompted her, "There are signs everywhere, all the time. When we are connected deeply, the frequency of interpretation of our signs increase. Follow the guide within you, and watch the divine design unfold in front of you. These indications are directions on our path in the inner world."

Once you have decided on the goal, we only need to remind ourselves of the commitment every day, and work towards it constantly. We require a clear mind—open, peaceful, connected—to achieve it.

She shared her thoughts with her husband, Jai, while they were on an unplanned weekend holiday in Lonavala. Isha understood that feeling happy and staying connected were synonyms. The goal was to be aware, to be a witness each moment. It took some time to differentiate which was Sai's voice and which was her mind talking, but once tuned in, it was easy to recognize the difference.

Isha shared the words that she had written—Drop your defences, be the beautiful person you truly are—in her yearbook when she was leaving college. "It is amazing how the same thoughts and words reverberated around me all the time."

Jai shared, "It is all ONE. All life is an exercise to interpret and then merge with the Divine."

She was probably being taught something.

"Ya," she repeated dreamily, "all life is Yoga. Life's aim is to meet the Lord within."

She lay down on the grass, drenched, with the diary in front of her witnessing the film in front of her.

She was scribbling in her diary...

All I need to learn, breathing right. Somehow that seems the most difficult thing to learn. Why do we rush to live? I wonder. This is not a one time lesson, learning and continual practice is the secret.

There are no boundaries in this experience, every breath is a new morning, a new year. It is all one. One energy… one truth …one existence….and my breath reminds me this… whenever i care to listen…

❀ ❀ ❀

8. One

*"Look closely at cloth, you see only threads.
Look closely at creation, you see only Self"*

— Ashthavakra Gita

Jai and Krish were playing carom this Sunday afternoon. Krish played skilfully and managed to flick the striker so as to put most of the carom coins in the pockets. Jai was struggling to keep pace with the young kid.

As Isha watched both of them playing with utmost attention and excitement, she thought, "It was like a game of carom. One thought from the inner world or shot from the striker and the entire arrangement of coins on the carom board changes. A small change in thought could simply redesign the entire outer manifestation."

Each mindset that we choose to have is like a metro station. We can choose to stay in the same mindset or metro station for as long as we want. We can choose to relax, condemn, indulge, or conform. It's up to us to decide to move on. We can choose to move on after lifetimes. Why is it such a big deal? It's not easy to change perspectives. A change of perspective is instantaneous, but that instant can take a lifetime to come.

Amazing…we have such a complete choice and we choose to see so little of it. The road is also amazingly well connected, each platform is connected to ourselves, our goal by the shortest route. Each of us has the choice to take this route whenever we choose.

Isha wondered why we stop and identify with these thought stations when it's so easy to just be.

We're probably so habituated to the outer world dramas of rushing, cribbing, pushing ourselves that we consciously choose to ignore to just Be. Could she choose to completely escape all these dramas she found herself to be a part of?

Krish was sharp and she felt that he read her emotions even before she had interpreted them. She had been discussing her Sai journey with him. He was always excited to hear her thoughts and experiences.

"Ma," he said, "you know, each one of us is connected. They are no middlemen needed and no rituals. We all have our own inner journey which is exciting."

She was happy to hear this. She loved him. He always added to her perspective.

Her son was reading the *Mahabharata*. The book was lying at his bedside. She picked it up to read. She randomly turned to a chapter titled 'Yudhishtra is dreaming.' A few sentences stood out: "Your days of exile are almost over. Go home. Leave dwaita vana." She wondered if the lines were saying something to her. Was this magic? She was surprised. How could the book hold exactly the lines she had been thinking about?

It was as if someone had told her to leave her dualistic (dwaita) perspective, and go to the true perspective; the place where we see ourselves as extensions of all beings.

Her inner Guru explained, "When we live only in the physical realm or have a dualistic perspective, we perceive the world through our senses and believe that the physical world is our sole reality. We see ourselves and all others separate from each other and have access to limited resources. From this perspective of lack, we begin to believe, for instance, that if someone else finds success or finds fame, riches or love, we might be left out. We become steeped in competition that pits us against one another and prevents us from experiencing true bliss. In truth, we are all one, belonging to the same all-pervasive spirit. Once we realise that we are completely connected, the notion of competition disappears giving way to cooperation and love. In this state, we know that when one person succeeds we all succeed. Also, all come together to complete me."

The *Mahabharata* and *Ramayana* are literary sojourns through the unexplored mental forests and learning of monistic truths and qualities of love, forgiveness and physical sacrifices that come along with it. We need to focus hard enough on it to see the lessons these stories can teach us. This is true for our life stories too.

Sai added, "Not only these, all the dramas that you have chosen to witness in any lifetime carry a message for you to reach the truth. These experiences are for you to understand, interpret and move ahead enriched by the lesson and experience."

Each day, each experience we have in our daily routine should be used as a lesson to help us in our inward journey.

"We could see the clearing of our thoughts similar to the process of cleaning our desk or cupboard. Raining from the skies could remind us of the universal love from the skies engulfing us. In this way, we could continue with our daily work while reminding ourselves of the perspective all along. This had to be a constant endeavour, a regular commitment."

The other problem Isha faced was weak will power. She would commit but still not do, even simple things that were required for taking care of her own body. This lack of commitment was not seen in her when it was a job for the outer world at work or home. Why did she not respect herself enough to take care of herself? She was unable to nurture her physical or mental self. What kept her away from realizing the truth that she now understood?

She concluded that she still thought that the outer world was more real probably, true and of greater significance than the Self within. She felt sad for herself and sad that the efforts of Sai were not reaping its complete benefits.

"Sai, how do you explain this phenomenon? I have procrastinated all my life, pushed away what I have always wanted to do. Why do I do that?"

"You postpone when your short-term goals are not aligned to your long term goals."

9. Mindfulness

"To the mind that is still, the whole universe surrenders"

– Lao Tzu

Isha realized that for her the outer world and its happenings were real that despite all logic and understanding, she still saw her life revolving around those concerns.

Why are you doing this to me?

Circumstances were as she saw them. She did not want to be obsessed with them. She did not want to be a part of them. It was okay to be present as a witness but not as an actor. She struggled so much to move out of these dramas. How was it that she was pulled back into them each time? What would it take Sai to move her out of these dramas permanently?

She knew it was up to her. She had to remember Sai all the time. The longing for Sai as Radha had for Krishna rendered all else meaningless. She was then a channel to the universal flow, the design woven, the river flowing, the melodious music playing. Work happened and she enjoyed it. She was at her creative best contributing to the fun happening around, just as a child would be a part of all the fun that happened around them.

But the moment she withdrew from this mould of completely surrendering to the present, and let the thought machine concentrate on everything but the present, she saw the chaos. She could see the amazing chaos of egos, emotions, fear, anger and dramas; the obsession of the mind and the diseases of the body. She now wanted to run off to another theatre so that she wouldn't see this… She did not realize that she saw this not because the dramas were being enacted but because she had tuned herself to the drama frequency. The whole idea was to fine-tune her mind radio so that it would be tuned to the 'surrender to the moment' frequency. This was not easy. Her radio had been tuned to this drama frequency since eons.. She also learnt that love, the only force that governed the universal laws, would help her fine tune to the higher frequency.

She discovered that the voice within always spoke to us, but often we did not give it our ear. The voice became softer till we are hardly able to hear it. We just needed concentrated effort in tuning ourselves. This voice was the knower of the truth—the one who revealed—the guide unto ourselves. We could never go wrong if we had the guide with us.

She felt happy with this phenomenon. Were these thoughts hers completely? Not as long as she considered herself as a separate person, the voice within answered.

"Gottcha!" Isha laughed to herself. Sitting at her desk, she watched the activity in the office with a faraway look.

10. The Inner Cleansing

Isha was sipping hot milk. She was now on this journey into herself and she was loving it.

She noticed she had stopped chewing her nails, a habit she had acquired early in her childhood. She had tried to break the habit numerous times but had never really succeeded.

She had always wanted something earlier. She used to think that these unending desires made life more interesting. But somehow the frequencies of these desires had decreased and also, fulfilment of all the mental fancies was also less important to her now. The body is only an instrument for a higher purpose— the realization of the Divine splendour that filled the Universe, of which we are a fraction. We had to use all the talents of your senses, intelligence, and memory for this goal.

Sai said, "Like the donkey that carries sandalwood without knowing anything more than its weight, you too carry the burden of the worldly worries, without being aware of the fragrance that you can get from the very burden on your back."

Desire leads to expectations and these unfulfilled expectations cause us hurt. Then, we fall back into the vicious mode of reacting instead of responding. Be a witness to the happenings around. Be still. It is amazing to see now how desires ruffle us, first mentally, then physically. It is a whirlpool of short term desire and joy in vicious cycles which goes on till we realize that we have spent our entire lifetime in these whirlpools, and instead, we could've chosen the option of enjoying and moving beyond to explore and grow.

Let go of your attachments to possessions. Do not depend on them to make you happy. There is no moment so beautiful as when you live happily, carefree, with no insecurities, no hoardings for security, by just being.

Let go of all the fears that grip you.

When you have access to the universal energy, when you know you have whatever you'll ever need, you are contended. When you know you are all energy and have access to the universal mind, when you know yourself to be the creator, would you desire more? You can only want more when you do not have. A person with universal consciousness cannot desire 'more' and rolls in this feeling of abundance and contentment.

When she had sat down to meditate some days ago, she had seen two ropes suspended from the sky. One rope led to Sai and the other led to the group of illusions/people she was creating all the time. She saw herself shift from the worldly rope and hold the Sai rope tight. Now, whenever she felt distracted by thoughts/emotions, she just imagined herself climbing the Sai rope and it would help. She had lately observed a loosening of the tied-up emotions.

When we submit our thought machine to the present moment, it stops being judgmental and work happens as if by itself. Our body and our mind become instrumental in the work that is happening.

Work happens best when we don't know it as work. The doer and the work merge into one. There was no separate consciousness beyond the work happening. We should work because we enjoy it d not because we need to reach, finish, achieve the goal. This is what results in stress because we concentrate on a future event that is not under our control.

Don't attach yourself to the failures either. Nothing has a hold over you until you allow it. Learn to let go. Don't identify yourself with your failures or your successes. Know that you are eternal. These failures are only lessons for you to learn so that they do not repeat themselves again.

She remembered Steven Covey and the lesson he had taught the world. Anticipating future events and results creates stress. Variables include time and results. Know your circle of influence!

There was only the 'Now' in which you could invest in. The dimension of time and space is the biggest illusion we need to cross before we can get close to the truth. The rush in our lives is because of this belief in the dimension of time. If we could just leave this behind, there would be only peace, no rush to reach. Distances and goals were illusions. All is here and now. There is always enough time. If we feel stressed running around, we need to identify the things that are really important for us in life. We need to make sure that we get rid of the things that consume our energy during the day. Stress is an external world concept and feeling. It is only possible to be stressed if your convictions in the external world manifestations and existence are so strong that you stop connecting with yourself. Why should we choose to do that?

11. Relationships

Isha had always been a mirror to the world. She had never realized that she was a lamp of cosmic beauty. She had surrounded this lamp with a mirror around it so completely that she had forgotten that a lamp lay within. She had always given back to the world the emotions she received. Reflecting and deflecting what she was surrounded with and given, she had never delved deeper to discover her true nature. Her defensive reactions had been a reflection of this attitude.

She realized the futility of identifying herself as a mirror which only reflected insecurities.

Isha realized that she had been a mirror all these years reflecting emotions, behaviour and attitudes that were directed towards her. She had never learnt that other people's behaviour could never be a reflection of her.

A person's behaviour could only be a reflection of their thought process and the circumstances they wished to create for themselves. She was not here to mirror the world's reflection. Instead, she was a beautiful independent source of cosmic energy. The lamp within her burnt alone, surrounded by the mirror which walled her from communicating with the lamp. Her communications were with the world outside as a mirror. A mirror only reflects the image of what is in front of it. That was what she reflected all the time. Her personality, her thoughts changed each moment. And at the end of the day, she could never figure out who she was or where she was going and why?

With Sai's help, she was cleaning up the glass to transmit the light of the lamp within.

Even though, all of us will reach the same goal, we all come from different perspectives. We are at different parts of our journey and therefore, unable to see each other's point of view.

Only the enlightened are able to understand how perfect the world is. Buddha had laughed when, after enlightenment, he understood that everything was just how it should be, nothing needed to be changed.

The inner world, the thought machine, can only revolve around the Self, the connect to the universal consciousness. Any other diversion /thought is an entry to the ego world which soon occupies the entire mind space. Therefore, it is so important not to submit to obsessive thoughts/strong emotions.

It is at times like these when it is so difficult, and yet so important, to move out to the middle path. It is at these times when it is so imperative to control the thought machine.

We need to understand that everyone might not be on the same journey at the same time.

There are people we meet and we feel we have known them for longer than we have known ourselves. There is no need for an introduction, no time taken to understand, a single meeting makes up for all the times you were not a part of each other's lives. At the same time, there are people we struggle to belong to for all the hours of the day, for years together and still do not feel understood. No matter how correct they look, if it does not feel right it is okay to move on.

The problem is when we bang our heads against the wall of our thought. This means that our belief systems and perspective needs to be worked upon.

Stepping back and working on herself was interesting. Every day she found situations to work on. Her triggers were similar and she concluded that she had gotten better. She was giving herself more time and everything around her seemed to be working better too.

"Isha, you have forgotten to turn the geyser off again," her husband called out from the bathroom.

"Why don't you switch it off if?" she snapped. She regretted getting annoyed even before she had completed her sentence.

Isha was surprised by how threatened she continued to feel when someone pointed out her shortcomings.

"Why did I feel so threatened?" she queried.

"Your lowered self- esteem, its probably because you concluded that the other person's truth is the only truth that exists. So, you tried to defend your actions," Sai explained to her.

Others do not create all the circumstances that we face. They were Our creations with the Divine, for our growth to self-realization. These circumstances are created so that we are given the opportunity to face our defences,

Isha was learning to work on herself. It was taking her longer than she had anticipated.

"Deep-seated habits, Sai,"she murmured to herself.

"You have to be constantly vigilant," Sai continued.

She remembered her habit of being defensive or stepping onto someone's space came at the most unexpected times, when she was really tired or low on energy.

But now, as she walked out of the habits that had chained her, she found a new release, a freedom. She loved the experience of exploring this new world. She felt like a warrior who had won a war, an explorer who had discovered new lands. There was a new sense of confidence, a sense of ownership about herself. She was now loving this journey into the unknown.

Now that she had learnt to look at herself as a spectator, she saw numerous flaws that needed correction. This knowledge did not make her agitated, rather there was quiet confidence and excitement to work on them. She wondered where this journey would take her. This seemed more exciting than the outer world gifts and competitions.

She no longer 'craved' for money, respect, promotions, recognition, fame, love and any other 'outer world' gift, but looked at it as an amused spectator.

There was a palpable energy, a light headedness, a conspicuous aura of love and joy around her which one could not miss.

A suggestion to improve herself brought a twinkle in her eye. She remembered her days of defensiveness and chuckled to herself.

She was now the sculptor who had to work on herself. Nothing could equal her sense of joy, contentment that she experienced each moment. She finally knew that she was on the right path.

Our thought, speech, and action have to be aligned for us to feel fulfilled and confident.

She noticed that whenever she found herself obsessed with a particular thought or a situation, she would pray for a connection with the voice within, the Self within. She noticed that the alignment to the Self within gave her greater inner strength, and the thought would soon relieve her from the obsession. Forgiveness or 'letting go' of memory also gave the beautiful gift of freedom and clarity of thought. When she spent time with older people, she realized they often needed a release of the baggage they held. We need to develop the habit of release, of letting go of thoughts that we might be carrying.

She knew she would not seek another's approval. Sai guided her with authenticity and clarity whenever she looked for direction. She had learnt to decipher when she was being guided by the other and when she felt depleted of energy.

Never feel disturbed by the other's concept of you. The other person might be seeing from dualistic glasses and misjudge you. The strength of your perspective should hold stable during these moments of challenge.

Still seeing Isha uncomfortable and full of questions, Sai explained, "There are people who may choose to use their thought machine differently. They may see things differently. But all thought machines are oiled by the same love. Send love to the other person. You could choose to stay there or move on. There is nothing that cannot be won over by love."

While driving to work this morning, she realised she had a crowded mind again. Surprised, she analyzed her thoughts and she realised that the root of their origin was fear.

'Sai, 'Isha called out within, asking for light again.

'Do the things you fear,' Sai shared, 'Make a list of all the things you are scared of. Fear is just negative baggage that we gather subconsciously. The only way to shed it is by facing fear. Doing what we are scared of.

"Here's a rose for you, Ria. It smells as lovely as you do'. Ria's smile, when she heard her mom, lit up her eyes. Isha smiled too. She had left office at lunch today and just entered home. 'Lets pack some chocolates, sandwiches and meet your Dad in the garden close to his office, Isha gushed. Krish and Ria were all excited and broke into an impromptu dance. Isha joined in after putting on their favourite song.

The park had fun rides too. They had never surprised their Dad in this manner and were excited about the surprise picnic.

The happiness that Isha felt within wanted expression. Her heart was filled with joy when she saw a picturesque sunset, a radiant flower, smelt sweet fragrance, heard a melodious song or gorged on some tasty food. She found herself indulging in these luxuries all the time now. She realised that she had earlier appreciated beauty only when she was on a long holiday. She now saw herself indulging in these beautiful luxuries all the time. These were not necessarily expensive.

They managed to call Jai outside his office and his surprised expression made their day.

'How did you come up with this idea,' Jai asked, knowing that this idea was not on her mind this morning when he left for office.

'Responding to my personal navigator within,' Isha shared. Jai had noticed that Isha was filled with fun and exciting thoughts these days and implementing them would lead to the most rewarding results.

Having spent her energy running around with the kids, she lay on the grass in a quieter corner to observe the beautiful sky.

She heard some noises in the far distance.

"How do you explain conflicts?' Isha was asking Jai. "No dialogue. Only love can see us through conflict to a resolution. A conflict arises when there are two different points of view. The same thoughts are viewed from polar perspectives. The universal consciousness has the correct design. At these moments, when you feel a conflict, dive within and surround yourself with love. The most important thing is to never respond in the heat of the moment. Things have a way of resolving themselves when we fill ourselves with love."

True dialogue asks for complete empathy. You be in my place and I be in yours. Often, no words can be spoken. Silence speaks the loudest. As thoughts are the inputs, our speech is the most important output. It is important that we learn to regulate it under all circumstances. Let your speech be the voice of the connect within, Isha concurred.

She was learning that everything was regulated with love.

"Isha, you and all beings are a treasure and such a treasure has to be cherished and celebrated.

You deserve all the good this world has to offer. When you know this, your outer world will reflect the thought that you are worthy of abundance and you shall attract all the gifts this universe has to offer.

She heard Sai whispering within, "The goal of self-realisation depends upon the foundation of self-confidence. You must, therefore, first develop confidence in yourself. Without having confidence in yourself, if you keep talking about the power being with someone else all the time, when are you going to acquire any power and confidence in yourself? You should consider self-confidence as the most important asset in life. Without self-confidence, you can never attain bliss. You are God yourself; God is the eternal resident of your heart."

This world was a reflection of the feelings she sent around her. The essence of life, Isha learnt, is to be centered within.

Isha got up early that morning. She got ready to go for a morning walk. The fresh air was really energizing. She always got immersed in beauty whenever she was with nature. There were leaves of various shapes, sizes, and colours. Each one was as beautiful as the other, as unique, as complete.

There is beauty in each leaf, in each vein. Beauty arises when you see the amalgamation, the totality, when you connect within. Otherwise you gather, hoping to see it in numbers.

"Why does everybody not see it as clearly?" Isha was asking Sai again.

"You don't force a new perspective on another. It is for them to choose," replied the voice within.

She saw a tree loaded with mangoes. We were so used to hoarding. The beauty of the external world was to be enjoyed but not hoarded. The thought and intention while giving were important. When you give, give because you are a part of the whole.

Recently, Isha had started recognizing all the situations in life that had been specifically tailor-made for her as tests to learn, clear, and move on to the next challenge. She no longer thought of the external world as unreal. It was the playground on which she had to encounter and pass her tests. This outer world and the situations she encountered were the examinations and progress reports. It indicated to her where she had reached.

Life was exciting now. She no longer thought negatively about the challenges that she encountered. The moment the challenge is understood and deciphered, it disappears as if it has never existed. You find yourself back to square one, identifying your next challenge.

Isha was scribbling in her diary before she went to sleep:

'Life is just a play. I am the actor, spectator, director, observer, participant, the creator and the created, the lover and the loved, the doer and the work, the teacher and the student on different planes of thought. I am the painter, the painted and the painting. I am the sculptor and the sculpted, the process and the clay, I am the admirer, the beauty, the essence. I choose to play different roles at different times. I choose to be all the roles at the same time. I choose to be none.

The idea is to surrender to the present moment by being happy, forgiving, non-judgmental. Give your best and move on. Carry no baggage whatsoever. You are the creator of love. Conflicts arise because of a lack of love for yourself, people, and things around you. Never feel depleted of this love. It is only a breath away. Connect within and remind yourself of this correct perspective and give. Do not recoil, give yourself away, work yourself away, and find happiness in the fact that you are this inexhaustible source. The more you tune yourself to the source, the more you connect, and the greater number of channels open for you to connect. Do not feel insecure. You are a boundless form of this energy. Your intention in each moment must be to give, to connect, and to drench yourself in Oneness…this energy, this perspective, the serenity, the peace, the happiness. Also, since you open yourself to the universe, the universe also opens itself to you. It becomes more willing to fulfil the desires that are in coherence with its design.

We need to create love.

We react adversely when we forget that we are the source that creates love. This energy is complete and second to none. If we can truly understand our beauty, our worth, we would not feel threatened by anyone. If we could give all our energy to the present moment, we would not have unresolved conflicts.'

Isha continued writing:

'A new day starts when the realization dawns, 'this is my life.' The thoughts in my life are my responsibility and are the beacon on my path of life.'

Since the time, Sai had come in and had helped unclog her thought machine, she felt clearer. She realized her immediate need to look at her thought machine. She discovered that discipline was a strong weapon with the help of which she could control her thought machine.

12. The Mind-Body Connection

"The secret of health for both mind and body is not to mourn for the past, worry about the future or anticipate troubles, but to live in the present moment wisely and earnestly."

— *Gautama Buddha*

Isha remembered what Sai had said earlier. He had said that there were two variables we received from outside, thoughts and food. These were like clay given to us to design ourselves, to sculpt, erase and sculpt again.

The guru had explained, "Both need to enter our body with awareness."

This body was a machine and needed exercise for optimal functioning.

She understood now. There were different levels: Physical world, the mental or the thought world, the energy world and others. These were all interconnected. Only when we are aware of the inputs into ourselves, we could be sure of the output. The energy that is connected with the food while it is being grown, cooked or eaten is also important. They are also interlinked with each other. Food influences our thoughts and our thoughts influence our food intake.

The food becomes me, my body, my thoughts. It becomes a variable on my path to myself. It is so important we connect within when we eat. The energy that we derive from food ultimately nourishes my physical body, defines my thought.

Isha was feeling a slight tinge of pain in her back.

"So! Once more you choose to fall ill," Sai remarked.

"Choose to fall ill?" Isha said indignantly.

"Why would I choose to do something so hurtful to myself?" She asked. "Why don't you believe me? Instead of helping me, you ridicule me."

She felt Sai smile affectionately within her. "It is your thoughts that make you feel healthy or otherwise. You haven't connected with me for the cleaning for some days now.

You probably thought that you don't need to do it for some time now. You imagined that the stray thoughts could be allowed for some days now and managed later. See how you love to trouble yourself," Sai explained.

"You mean I can think myself out of it."

"Yes…that is the only rule," Sai confirmed.

It is so important to stay tuned in to ourselves with each breath and each posture, each thought, each moment. If we were aware of how we breathe, our posture, and our thoughts, it would be constant meditation or pranayama in action.

"Health is the fundamental requirement to achieve a goal. Otherwise, we will not be able to keep our mind strong and clear. It is so interconnected. The body houses the mind, and the mind manifests the body. Both influence each other. If we take care of one, we start to take care of the other," Sai shared.

She saw, 'dis' 'ease" was also due to disharmony. Since the time she had started looking within, she could often trace the disharmony within her, when she fell ill. They were many reasons for an illness which she couldn't explain yet but she knew even when there were external causes for illness, our high energy levels could raise our immunity and thus make the 'dis' ease more bearable.

The more Isha looked at her body, the more she realized that the body was a grosser manifestation of the thought process. As our negative thoughts become concrete, they start manifesting in the form of disease. As the volume of the thought increases, depending on how often we chose to let our mind repeat them to us, how many times we chose to hear the repeated thought, the kind of negative thought, they start manifesting in the grosser body.

She understood that the universe was an unending source of energy and that we needed to draw from it.

Our thoughts could often deplete us of that energy and create physical illness. This also tells us something about the strength that our mind possesses.

We can manifest our thoughts physically. Wow!

If we have been given this precious mind machine, why do we let it rule us? Why don't we realize this thought machine is there to help us? Why don't we screen the thoughts that we put into the machine for it to repeat and manifest?

Isha remembered the words she had read in the *Gita*. She had always thought of Arjun as body Consciousness and Krishna as Universal consciousness.

Enthralled by the prospect of divine understanding, Isha asked Sai to explain further with his enlightening words. She now heard Sai explaining, *"Always remember you are the dweller, not the body. You are the one who wears the cloth; you are not the cloth itself. You are the resident of the house. You are the witness, the knower of the individual. But now, you are mistaking yourself to be the limited individual. Eventually, all the momentary pleasures and enjoyments will turn into sorrow. Keep your mind steady and discharge your duties, remembering your atma. Do not think or worry about birth and death, or the joy and sorrow which accrue to you. Birth and death are relevant only to the body. They do not refer to you. You are not the body. You are the permanent entity which is free from birth and death. You have neither beginning nor end.*

You were never born and will never die. Nor will you ever kill anyone. You are the atma. You are all pervasive. Verily, you are God. Your very self is God and God is you."

Her mind was at peace now. Isha sat for a while in a state of intense divine tranquillity.

13. Surrender

"Music in the soul can be heard by the universe"

– Lao Tzu

"I submit all my perceptions to you—my sense of time, distance, existence. I submit to you," Isha prayed that morning.

When we surrender, we surrender our thought machine to him for cleaning so that we can be completely present in the moment. Thanks, Lord, for the beauty granted.

"You must develop this attitude of 'merging' with the divine in all that you do, this attitude of dedication and surrender to His Will. This is the best means of realizing Him,"

"Mummy, but there is no God," Krish, her 10-year old son, argued, "my teacher has explained to us this."

"True, my dear," she said, "Your teacher is right. There is no God as a separate entity from all that we already know, but I have always found it easier to see a physical form as an embodiment of universal consciousness.

Nothing changes, it only helps me converse better and submit more easily to the universal consciousness. HE has helped me since I first connected with him. I feel lighter. He hears, guides, caresses, and loves me. He never lets me stray. Life has more meaning. He is there in the deepest of my thoughts—feeling, guiding, holding my burden, cleaning me of any thought he does not approve of. A feeling of pure love sweeps over you when you completely surrender. I feel secure. I know He is eternal and shall never abandon us, not in the time or distance dimension." Isha explained

Isha was thankful that Sai had decided to work upon her. "But, why me?" she had asked.

"Oh, its everybody who chooses to connect, to talk to me, anybody who surrenders his thought machine to the universal consciousness," the Master shared.

Sai continued to dissect Isha whenever and wherever he chose. He was asking Isha about the dramas in her office and her obsession with them.

"Why, when you have seen the steadiness of relationship with Me, would you chose to upset yourself with frivolous incidents in your daily life.? Why are they more real for you than My relationship with you?" he hammered her again.

Sai, the shepherd, continued, "What a devotee was Radha! She was always looking for Krishna, always talking about Krishna, always thinking about Krishna. There was not a moment when Krishna was not in her mind, in her consciousness. She was looking for Him, singing to Him. Even when she slept, she had no other dream but about Krishna. What a wonderful devotee was Radha!"

Isha now understood. It was now her responsibility to be steadfast in the truth which had been revealed to her.

'Who is there to love?

To give to?

To compete with?

To hurt or be hurt by?

It's only Me wherever I see.'

Life is beautiful when we surrender. It is amazing to see the baggage we carried all these years for no reason. Here, there are no other goals or prizes other than HIM. So, there is no stress.

Life isn't easy until you surrender completely. The relationship between a mother and a child, a teacher and a student, a boss and employee, a husband and a wife could be examples of complete surrender in this physical world. A single-sided surrender leads to power struggles,

Isha scribbled in her diary:

Know that the design is much grander than we can ever conceive. 'I wish to reach that degree of surrender where He is the only identity.'

❀ ❀ ❀

14. Being with Sai

"A good traveller has no fixed plans, and has no intent on arriving"

— Lao Tzu

The teacher and the taught were one. She was now sharing her thoughts more often with people around her. She felt so complete when she spoke and was truly amazed at the words that came out. These did not feel like her conscious thoughts. It was as if she stood aside as a witness when the words flowed through her. Whenever she sat with Sai, she felt a sense of catharsis. She felt lighter. Unasked questions were answered and unframed thoughts fell into place.

There is nothing small or big. There is no 'other' in this world. The need to control...compete...to reach does not exist.... There is no past or future in this presence. There is only beauty...awareness...lightness...only happiness in this experience of the present moment.

Isha, *you reside in ME. This body of yours and everything you see or perceive resides in this universal consciousness. The only way to truly live is to know that I am all consciousness who can choose to manifest in any form. You and I are one. The correct way to live is to be in this awareness always and let your mind and body be an instrument to this awareness. In this manner, you will do only what the universal consciousness desires.*

If we truly knew we were this priceless treasure, would we really want less? Would we want to be small and limit ourselves? We are precious, unique, complete. Why did we slip from this truth, this perspective? Why do we not hold on to this concept always?

"Isha, do you know, it is possible to know and talk about the truth and still not believe it or live it? If we consume ourselves with an outer display of scriptural wealth, there is no time left inward to dive for priceless pearls."

The real pilgrimage is to practice what you preach.

She understood what Sai was saying. The entire journey with Sai would be a waste if she did not practice what she had learnt with him.

When we drown ourselves in the beautiful sea of the unknown, for the first time we leave drudgery and negativity behind. We enjoy floating in the waves of the Lord's love, the soft movement of happiness.

"Isha, it has been a pleasant journey sharing my secrets with you. Thanks for opening up to me and being such a nice audience," Sai said quietly.

"You sound as if you are leaving. Please stay with me…," Isha pleaded, "I need a constant reminder to this perspective. Will I be able to walk alone within without you around?"

Isha was almost in tears now.

"I am always there with you. I shall appear in whatever form you desire to see me. I will be present always in the form of words, inspirations, a person, a dream, a thought, a voice. Whenever you wish to see me and whenever you call for me without pretensions, I will be with you," Sai consoled her.

Though she had been with Him for such a short time, Isha was now so dependent on his presence that she could not think of Him going away.

Her eyes fell upon a sentence in the newspaper she had been reading, 'The only real failure in life is not to be true to the best one knows.' She knew now that even though she might not have manifested the Thought completely, she was on the path of discovery. The journey only grew more beautiful and ecstatic as she delved into it. She knew she had access to this knowledge within her always and she saw herself more at peace. She felt more relaxed and this reflected in her health, confidence, self-esteem, relationships and her work. This thought machine had actually been given to support the inner voice so that we could pursue what we were born for.

❀ ❀ ❀

15. Seaside Reflections

Isha was on vacation, sitting by the shore, watching the waves form from water and dissolve therein. Watching the waves at play always transferred her to another world as if the waves had a story to tell. There is no unchartered sea. There are no mishaps. You encounter situations you have to learn from and move on in your journey. You are there as a channel to share and pass on knowledge. Each of us hears their own inner voice. It's just that we don't realise that this is the guiding voice in our journey of life. This journey is to acknowledge and understand this inner voice and let it guide us on the journey ahead.

Now, Isha observed all the structures within her collapsing. All the notions she had collected and built up were no more. She saw herself transform into a plane, moving across the skies and clouds and sunlight. It was a beautiful experience. There was nothing else she could see even though she tried to stare down. There was only purity and beauty of nature as far as she could she.

She was writing in her diary again:

'Here on vacation…I had to learn never to forget again…

These waves are like our bodies, emerging and manifesting themselves for that short while. When they jump and dance and shine in their full bloom, and then after having spent their time and energy, some bigger, mightier and stronger than the others, they slow their pace down until they all merge into each other eventually.'

I wonder if the waves know when they were born or when they were jumping. I wonder if they know that they actually were water only and they will return to their original form…

I wonder whether they compete amongst themselves as to which is bigger or bubblier or stronger. I wondered if they knew what mattered was only what mattered to them…

I wonder if they know that once they return to the ocean, they might not have any memories of what they had been moments earlier.

I wonder if they will realise that there was never any competition. They came from the ocean and they will return to it.

Eventually, nothing mattered.

Nobody could take away their beauty…their essence from them…

They were whatever they identified themselves to be…

whatever they chose to be…

The waves who were born to die and had no choice of their own…

The glorified beauties who danced in the sunshine with frothy white dresses to adorn them.

The ocean itself…

It was up to them.

They also understood that the joy in their lives would be what they identified themselves to be…

Whatever they think dissipated in the water…

What they would see around was what they saw themselves as….

The fame, money, and diamonds were the transient froth the waves wore…

It was ok to enjoy all as long as you knew that you were a wave in the ocean.

You always were,

The Journey Within

You always are,

You shall always be,

I roll in the waves of this awareness…from one dimension to the other…they merge…I see only Me around. The sea is ME. The waves are Me. I stand and see the waves.

❀ ❀ ❀

www.ingramcontent.com/pod-product-compliance
Lightning Source LLC
Chambersburg PA
CBHW061248140726
47998CB00006B/2143